Jumpstart For Business
Turn Your Slow Months into Your Best Months

Angel Tuccy

Copyright © 2017

Jumpstart for Business; Turn your slow months into your best months

Angel Tuccy

Website: www.JumpstartForBusiness.com
Twitter @JumpstartForBusiness
Facebook: Facebook.com/JumpstartForBusiness

ISBN-10: 978-1976054495
ISBN-13 978-1976054495

BISAC: New Business Enterprises, Small Business & Entrepreneur

Jumpstart™ is a unique and systematic approach to helping small businesses create profit all year long.

All Rights Reserved.

Jumpstart For Business

"Most business plans includes everything needed to start and grow your business, except for one crucial thing, how to build a great customer base."

Table of Contents

Chapter 1	Jumpstart System	11
Chapter 2	Who You Know	15
Chapter 3	Plan for Success	27
Chapter 4	VIP Specialist	47
Chapter 5	Visibility Cloak	63
Chapter 6	Invitation Marketing	73
Chapter 7	Follow Up Stage	89
Chapter 8	Radio Star	97
Chapter 9	Share Kindness	107
Excerpt	Lists That Saved My Business	109

As an entrepreneur, you get to work half days:
7am until 7pm.

You get to create a legacy,
Out of your garage.

The dreams that get you excited,
Scare most of the people you know.

When you take a call on your vacation, it isn't work,
You love what you do.

When you love what you do,
You'll never work a day in your life.

Chapter 1
Jumpstart System

I started the day pretty excited. I jumped out of bed as soon as the alarm went off, something I've had to really train myself to do. I made my bed before leaving my room. I read through my calendar and morning devotional while multi-tasking in the kitchen. I'm an optimist, so this also means I struggle with leaving on time. I always think I have more time to do just one more thing: empty the dishwasher, do a load of laundry, start the crockpot, or scroll through Facebook for "just a quick minute." Grabbing my computer bag, my lunch sack, my gym bag and my purse, I grab my haul and I'm off to start the day.

This is how most mornings go. I'm on autopilot. I've made my to-do list the night before, and my calendar rules the day. I imagine, you have the same routines most mornings, and most days start to blur into one another. Your business has developed its own habits, too.

Even if you haven't formalized it, your business has systems that have gotten you to right where you are right now. You have a ritual for your daily habits. You have a crowd of people you hang out with, networking, or brainstorming, or binging on social media. You have your typical sales process that you can probably recite in your head and before you go into any meeting, you already can anticipate what the outcome will be.

At night, I crawl into bed, exhausted. Working so hard, giving so much to everyone around me, and wanting so much to provide a great resource for small business owners, my body ached for them. I'd meet with business owners everyday that were working to take their business to the next level but feeling like there's so much competition working against them. Even though they were making a lot of money, they really weren't that profitable. Their batteries, and mine, were running dry. We were at risk of burnout. We needed a Jumpstart!

Going out to my car, I put my key in the starter, and nothing happened. My car's battery was dead. Everything that was on autopilot immediately came to a halt. All of my priorities shifted. All my attention was on getting my car started so I could get going.

Enter my breakthrough moment. I hope you have a breakthrough moment while reading this book, too. That no matter how fast you're going, everything can change, if you choose it to. Your business can be on the brink of closing down, and one great opportunity can turn it around.

One great idea that you haven't thought of before can be the turning point to create a more profitable business. Your next power partner can be at the next networking event you go to. Your next social post can be viewed by just the right influencer. It can all happen quickly. When you're open to success and to opportunity, it shows up.

You have to pay attention to the people you hang out with and to the television shows you watch, the books you read, and especially to the stuff you say when you talk to yourself.

It all sets you up for success or for burnout.

Giving your business a Jumpstart™ can turn your slowest months into your best months. It can bring in new energy for those great new clients, and it can be the reminder that there are probably a few things you're doing that you shouldn't be. If your calendar is filled with "busy", stop the madness and fill it with productive items that move you closer to your goal *every day*. Not just once in awhile, every single day.

The Jumpstart™ System reminds you that you can give your business a boost anytime you need one.

When you put the Jumpstart™ System in your calendar, you'll find that your slow months turn into your best months. Get away from being on autopilot, and infuse some quick techniques that excite and you remind you why you truly love being an entrepreneur.

Chapter 2
Who You Know

You are sitting on a goldmine. You have an existing list of contacts, a database, maybe even an old list of people you've sent Christmas cards to. According to an age-old survey of wedding planners and funeral directors, the average person is tightly connected to 250 people. In a short amount of time, you can combine your social media accounts with all your other lists of names, and you've got a great database to work with. Your existing database is a goldmine to tap into for creating excitement, awareness, and bringing fresh revenue into your sales process.

Cold Leads

You have a stack of business cards of prospects that are no longer hot leads because the follow up process has taken too long to turn into a sale.

Don't give up on this list.

Today's numbers tell us that a prospect can take up to 15 follow up activities before they buy from you. Fifteen.

The average sales person only follows up with a warm or hot lead three times, which means, you've got a lot of potential business sitting in your stack of cold leads.

However, after a few follow up phone calls for emails, it starts to feel like you're stalking, or worse, wasting everyone's time, but that's not usually the case. A majority of the time, the prospect is just as busy as you are, chasing down their own leads, and working in their own business. You may even be on *their* list of people to call, but other priorities take over, and you get pushed to the back burner. Remember, the ball is *always* in your court to follow up with the prospect, even if you left them with messages to contact you.

Action Step: Gather up your stack of business cards from people who haven't done business with you yet. This stack has tremendous value in turning your slow months into your best months.

I invited a prospect out for coffee to discuss a new project I was working on, and during the meeting, we discovered that she's been keeping an eye on my company's success for 2 years. 2 years! She finally decided to jump in and become a customer. During those last 2 years, I did more than just send her emails or newsletters, I'd reach out occasionally and invite her to join me at an event I was attending, or something I was up to. She didn't usually attend, but it allowed me to stay connected and keep my brand fresh and top-of-mind until the timing worked for her own needs.

So often, because we have our own goals and agenda to meet, we lose focus of the prospect's timeframe. They're busy closing their own deals and working on their own deadlines to care about serving yours. They're not trying to be rude, but just like you have to do; they've got to take care of themselves first.

When the timing is right, the timing will be perfect. The downside to a long and lengthy follow up process is being sure your brand is remembered, and the future sale isn't lost to your competition because you didn't stay connected. The Jumpstart For Business system™ will keep you far more connected then your competition and they won't be able keep up.

Previous Customers

Your previous customers are an incredible source for more business. Too often, we falsely create a longer repeat-sales cycle than is necessary. A local pizzeria encourages their customers to come back the very next day by saying, "See you tomorrow" at the end of each transaction. An international coffee company encourages their customers to come back later the same day by giving them a coupon with their morning java.

A local used-car salesman was having the worst month he'd ever had and called on us to help turn it around. A quick Jumpstart™ was all he needed and he made a few quick sales that gave him the confidence and the energy to keep going.

Taking the time to reconnect with previous customers is always a good use of time.

Even if you delegate this task to a virtual assistant or someone on your team, staying in touch with past customers is key to creating a sustainable business.

There are no guarantees that any of your previous customers will ever call on you again.

Right now, your previous customers are somebody's current prospect and while they're in the prospecting phase, they're being charmed away from doing business with you again.

However, you can create loyalty, but it doesn't happen by sending out a weekly newsletter.

Action Step: Implement a system for keeping track of your customers, including their buying habits and interactions you have with them. A cloud-based system allows for everyone on your team to have access to their contact information and buying data. Be sure that you aren't the only one on the team keeping track of this information, and be especially sure that you aren't trying to memorize it all. Get this information out of your head and into a piece of software.

Systems build businesses. You can train someone to follow your system, which allows you to stay focused on your highest priorities. If you're a sole-proprietor, you're handling every role in your company, and stalling your own progress. Systems will allow you to "fire" yourself from handling all of the administration, operations, bookkeeping, human resources, invoicing, scheduling, placing orders, stuffing envelopes standing-in-line, waiting-on-hold, and more.

Loyal Customers

In every business, there are a percentage of customers who love you.

They love your product, they tell people about you. They show up on time and they pay you on time. They don't squabble over every line item and they're quick to jump into every new thing you offer. They share your social media posts, and they write glowing reviews for you. They are your VIP's.

VIP's will continue to do business with you even if they move further away. Be sure to treat your VIP's with extra-special attention, and they will always out-perform you marketing dollars for you.

The challenge with getting your VIP's to continue to cheerlead for you is you feel like you have to keep creating new and exciting things for them to talk about. You start to feel like you have to continue to add new products or services, keep adding more value into the bundles you already have.

In my company, we had a 3-year period where we just kept adding and adding value, but the price-point didn't change. The workload kept increasing, but the profitability kept diminishing. At one point, we were offering a full-year business membership that cost my company $750.00 to run, and we were only charging the client $600.00. Because of volume, it took us over a year to realize we were going backwards.

The cost of continually adding new products can add up, and if you're struggling with a slow month, the profit to create something new won't always be there. You don't always need a new product to get your VIP's excited; you often just need a new way to share it.

The Jumpstart™ method will give your VIP's a non-stop system for referring you over and over again.

Your Sphere of Influence

Look in your phone and you'll discover you probably have about 250 people you could call or text right now and they'd respond to you. Your sphere of influence is bigger and greater than you probably imagine it to be.

We often feel more invisible than we really are but your life is making an impact on all those people, far more than you realize.

The realization of your impact doesn't happen by looking at the number of likes on your most recent social post, it comes in the form of cards in the mail, one-on-one conversations, and private messages. It comes when you reach out to someone and ask for help. It comes when you realize someone you know is struggling and you take the time to reach out to him or her privately. You're making an impact and sometimes they'll take the time to tell you, and sometimes, you need to hear it from a stranger. You'll find what you're looking for, and when you pay attention to the responses, you'll see your influence having an impact all around you.

I like to call your sphere of influence your FRANC circle. FRANC is an acronym to remind you of all the people you have a true connection with.

F – Friends
R- Relatives
A – Associates
N – Neighbors/Networks
C - Customers

Most of the people in your FRANC circle have no idea what you're up to or how they can help you grow. By keeping them in the loop, they can help you turn your slow months into your best months.

People You Haven't Met Yet

This is where it starts to get really great.
Everyone you know, knows people you don't know. Common sense, yes, but even though your business foundation may be built on your own personal connections, the sustainability will come from people who don't yet know about you.

You need people to follow you. You need market share. And you won't have the months and years that you've spent developing your current relationships to get this new crowd of people to trust you, so you need a quick and easy way to build credibility. People make snap judgments about people they don't know, so in order to develop quick rapport, we're going to show them how connected you already are to each other. We're going to remind them of how much you already have in common through your existing social connections.

You now have a working database; a great list of people who will soon be going through your system and creating more sales and revenue during your driest months. When you combine all your contacts together, you'll find there are a lot of people who haven't heard from you recently. There's a great resource of referrals ready and waiting for your marching orders. Let's give them something to share.

Chapter 3
Plan for Success

What makes one person so adept at accomplishing more than every one else around? How do they figure out everything that needs to be done, and actually manage to fulfill it?

The difference is planning.

People who succeed don't get there by accident. They plan for success, and they don't mess around. It doesn't mean that they're work-a-holics and never take time for fun. They work hard and they play hard.

When they write down their goals, it's not a one-time, write-it-down-stick-it-in-a-drawer-and-hope-it-comes-true type of success plan. It's a working, living, breathing document.

I admit, for 25 years, I carried around my Franklin planner and devoted time each and every day planning out my days, week, months, and yes, even years. Nothing happened until I first put it in the calendar.

I used my calendar as a journal, goal setting and to ensure that my checklists got checked off. I made checklists and the most important items on the list ended up on my calendar with a time and date to accomplish them. I never left home without my planner. It was as much a part of my outfit as my shoes. Every few years, I'd update the binder and give my planner a new style. Every October, I'd be as excited as a child at Christmas time when I'd head into the store to purchase next year's refill.

I'd read magazine articles on time-management and I'm a sucker for any title that starts with a checklist of "5 Ways to ..." I love being organized and ready for the events of the day.

I am surprised by the behavior of dear friends of mine who don't write anything down. I'm amazed that they don't consult a calendar and yet manage to keep their appointments. I admit, if I don't write it down, I will not remember it. My brain has trained me to write it down in order to remember anything.

I am further surprised at how often I meet someone who doesn't have a single goal written down. With everything that we know about the habits of highly successful people, why in the world aren't people writing down their goals?

Being spontaneous and creative have their place in experiencing the joy of life. Waking up in the morning and going where the wind blows you sounds so romantic and exotic. Traveling to distant places with only your backpack and a compass make for great stories and a lifetime of memories. More vacations are definitely in my plan.

In my circle, having a lifestyle where people aren't depending on you to bring home a regular paycheck is pretty foreign. I'm still in the growing and accomplishing phase so I need a schedule. I need a plan.

For small business owners, entrepreneurs, network marketers and commission-sales people, your livelihood requires that your hours aren't wasted, and in fact, are spent bringing more customers through your sales process. But do you know how many more? Without a written goal of what you need to accomplish, the chances of hitting your mark is fairly inconsistent, to be polite.

Write down this phrase: I own a multi-million dollar enterprise. Say it out loud. Saying it out loud should make your toes tingle. Your business is going to produce serious revenue. You're not running a hobby anymore.

You have a multi-million dollar company sitting at your fingertips, even if the bank deposit doesn't reflect it, yet. YET. Mind you, it's not about the money, it rarely is. It's about your mindset. Whether or not the dollars are important to you, you need to treat your company, and your time, as if you're running a thriving enterprise. Otherwise, well-meaning friends, television and the latest gaming app will distract you.

You'll put off making phone calls or setting appointments if you don't have the mindset to take your business seriously. If you work at home, you'll stay in your slippers far too long and then decide that you've stayed home this long, you might as well wait until tomorrow to get anything finished.

For my calendar-loving friends, who set up sales goals and track them throughout the month, even down to the day, you a strong force of nature on your side that can't be discounted. The math is built in for success. The calendar breaks easily down into four cycles of thirteen weeks each. By creating a sales plan for 12-weeks, each quarter gives you a gift of an extra week.

You can use this week for bringing your team together to create strategies. You can turn this week into a holiday or a bonus-trip for hitting your sales goals. You get to design your own lifestyle, and the calendar builds it in for you.

The tricky part to running a sales plan according to the month is that some months have 23 working days, and others may only have 19 or 20.

The secret to sales management is surviving the months with only 19 working days. That's where a 12-week sales-plan takes over. By planning your marketing calendar by the quarter and breaking it down to weekly goals, you create momentum, and sustainable activities to carry your team through the year.

I need more customers today!

Now you're thinking that you definitely need more customers. Let me tell you this. You don't need MORE customers.

You're thinking, "Yes, I do".

I hear it all the time, "I need more customers".

Okay, let me ask you, how many more? The answer can't just be MORE. How will you measure MORE? Is one more customer enough? Is it 10% more? 20%? Write down your real goal.

How many do you have now? Probably more than you know. Is every person in your database a current customer? Do you know how often they shop with you?

The key to hitting a goal is having a goal.

Before you begin the new sales week, you have to know what you want it to look like at the end of the week. It's your roadmap. It's your guide. It's your measurement against how close or far you are from getting there.

It's also your motivation.

When you see that you're 75% closer, your adrenaline kicks in. Your energy increases. You're focused. You're determined. You know you can do it. You've seen what it takes to get this far and you can duplicate it.

In October 2008, an associate suggested that we start a radio program. Recording audio programs and podcasting them on the Internet was beginning to trend and anyone with a cellphone and an Internet connection was becoming the host of their own radio show.

Internet radio was the new "brochure" for your business. Much like writing a book is a gateway for your company, that's how podcasting Internet shows were being promoted back then.

I say back then, as if nine years ago was so significant, but the Internet changes everything so lightning fast. We were fortunate to be in that wave.

Nine months after starting our podcast show, we switched from Internet to (what they call) terrestrial radio. This is what you have in your car. You can listen to our show on your AM dial. For the most part, our business model stayed the same. We continued to offer business training and business consulting, while hosting a 30-minute daily talk show on the AM dial.

We set new business goals, and having a radio presence increased our credibility. You could tune in and listen to us every single day and the message was the same as our business training. During the next 15-months, our business steadily increased, and we were able to publish a couple of books. Even though the business model was stable, a significant shift was taking place. We began to dream bigger.

The most significant change wasn't what our business model was doing; it was our dream for what our business model could be. From the very first day of broadcasting on the AM dial, a dream was triggered.

My background wasn't public speaking. I was never on the main stage like my co-host, Eric Reamer. Eric traveled the globe entertaining and teaching for fifteen years before I met him. Eric took me under his wing and helped me to become a public speaker. I started out quivering and shaking, with butterflies that refused to fly in formation, and began a speaking career that I am now deeply in love with. They say the best way to get over a fear is to face it and that's how it happened for me.

In those early days, I was a trembling, nervous wreck whenever I stood in front of an audience. I had no idea that I could hold on a conversation or speak to a group about a helpful topic. Fast forward the clock and I'm on the public radio every single day, and regularly speak in front of crowds ranging from small classrooms to large conferences.

The first day on the air imparted a brand new goal that had never existed before. The new goal for both of us was immediately born to become nationally syndicated radio hosts of a 3-hour daily program. Granted, that's a long ways away from the starting point of being a 30-minute program on one station.

That's the beauty of a goal. It doesn't matter where you're starting from, your starting point will be the impetus for inspiration. The greatest success stories are filled with failure and humble starting points in life. Take heart and know the worse off you are, the better your story will be. You have nowhere to go but up and the only thing standing between you and success is if you think you can't do it. Of course you can do it.

Of course you can do it. Believe in yourself. And when you feel like you don't have the belief, listen to those who believe in you more than you believe in yourself until you get to the place where you can say out loud, "Of course I can do it."

Goal Setting is the Simple Act of Writing Down What You'd Like To Do

Simple goal-setting starts with writing down things you'd like to do, places you'd like to see and whatever is on your mind that you haven't accomplished. Take however much time you need. This isn't the sort of exercise you accomplish in one sitting. This is a forever and on-going list. Each day will bring new ideas and new adventures to your mind. Keep a running tab on all of them. Make sure you add, "Turn my company into a multi-million dollar enterprise" to the list. Remember, it's not as much about the money as it is about creating the mindset that you are the CEO of a thriving company.

Writing down personal goals is the hardest part of all of this.

Too often, adults have lost the ability to dream big. I mean really dream big. The *"nothing is impossible"* big stuff. The downside to growing up is the realization that comes with dreaming. You know that each goal requires money and maybe talent and all the other excuses that never got in the way when you were a child and you thought you really could be Batman®. The easy route is to stop dreaming, and that's what most people do.

The people who hit top sales goals for their company, who accomplish the most in a given 24-hour day, are those who dream big.

Breathe some life back into those dreams again. Pat yourself on the back and set yourself towards the path that says, "I can do this".

Time Frame / Action Steps / Deadline

For your sales goals, take each individual goal and assign a time frame, deadline and the action steps to make it happen.

Input the action steps into your calendar. I am most productive in hitting sales goals when I start my week with sales appointments already set. This week, even if I'm busy, I am setting appointments for next week. This keeps me from riding the sales process rollercoaster.

When I look at my calendar and see the multiple meetings that bring in revenue are already set in my calendar, I know it's going to be a productive week.

I start the week on a high note and even if some of those meetings get rescheduled, or one or two don't go as planned, I know that that I have several others keeping me motivated.

You have goals to meet each and every day, or maybe in your line of work, your goals are monthly. The process is still the same, no matter what your deadline is.

When your goals are written down, and your action steps are in your calendar, you can let the time-wasters stop gaining traction. Each minute, the clock is ticking. When you're at work, each minute is precious and the time it takes you hit your goals is finite. You don't have an eternity. In fact, you don't have the luxury of putting off until tomorrow what you can do today. The lie we all tell ourselves is that there's always more time and it's okay to delay. That's not true. Today is all you truly have. The thing is, you know what you need to do. You know when you need to do it. Stop wasting precious time and get to it. Of course you can do it.

In general, the worse case scenarios only happen in your head. You are your worst critic and the biggest procrastinator and there's no good reason for it. You have a calendar. You have the goals for success written down. You have deadlines. Don't play small. Go out and grab that dream for yourself. No one else will. No one else will make your dreams a priority.

The Cheshire Cat in *Alice In Wonderland* told Alice that as long as she didn't care where she was going, it didn't matter which route she took. The same philosophy is true with your plans. If you don't have any action steps or deadlines, then you won't be able to track and measure growth. You won't realize just how close you are, or how far off track you really are.

Action Step: Look at your calendar for last week. How many of those activities were tightly connected to achieving your goals? How many things do you do first thing in the morning (once starting your work day) are moving the dial towards your success? Your daily habits will create huge success. Review and recalibrate your activities to schedule your goal-achieving activities everyday before letting the busy-work and other people's emergencies win your day.

Set The Bar Higher

My friend Ron wanted to help raise money for charity. He set forth a challenge to help raise funds, but rather than say he was raising money, he put an actual figure to the challenge. His challenge was to raise $1,000.00 for this fundraiser.

By establishing a clear dollar amount, everything raised was measured against the goal. As the donations increased, it was easy to share how close he was and motivation increased when they celebrated milestones along the way. You can rally the troops to keep going once they've hit the halfway mark. Others will step up to help when they see that you're close to accomplishing the target.

If Ron would've said, "I'd like to raise some money for this charity," he could have been satisfied when they raised $400.00. With four hundred dollars already earned, where is the incentive to keep going? When you set a goal to chase an unknown factor, the end-result causes you, and others around you to feel let down. You know you can do more, but without having a clear incentive, you allow the unknown factor to cause more damage than good.

By clearly setting the marker, you keep the motivation and measuring progress is built in.

Can you overshoot and blow your goals out of the water by totally exceeding them? You bet you can! The key is to continue to set a new goal along the way. If you hit your $1,000 charity goal early on, you can increase the goal to by 50%. If you hit that with enough time before the deadline, you can increase it again by 50%. You're never working against an unknown factor.

Set your business goals. Write them down. Give them a deadline and work the action steps to accomplish them.

Believe That Anything Is Possible

When Eric and I taught Experience Pros University, each student took an oath of commitment that carried him or her past the initial excitement phase, when work really starts to feel like work and you want you to go back to your old habits.

No Excuses
Believe That Nothing Is Impossible
Commit to Showing Up

In your business, writing down your goals is the first step to committing to them.

Eliminate any excuses, and surround yourself with people that believe in you.

Chapter 4
VIP Specialist

Not every person you interact with is a potential client. The truth is, sales is not a numbers game and every *"no"* does not lead you closer to a *"yes"*. Who was the brainchild behind the messaging that fed us that time-wasting line? The world of bringing in new clients and increasing revenue is a tough one. There are a hundred things you would rather do than pick up the phone and ask one more stranger if this is a good time for them. Knocking on strangers doors and making unsolicited phone calls is a terrible job, admittedly by anyone who's ever had to bring back a stack of business cards to their manager or dial-for-dollars off a list that was found in some archaic database.

One of the students who took our course later wrote us a testimonial, "Eric and Angel saved my sole." He was referring to the sole of his shoe. He used to wear out a pair of shoes every six months.

His job as the salesperson for his company was to knock on doors.

He would go door-to-door soliciting his service. He was given a geographic area that his company was targeting and hit the pavement. He was a pro. He enjoyed his job and he felt like he was good at it. He would wear out the sole of his shoes by putting in so many miles.

When we looked at the sales numbers and identified where new business came from, it was determined that 20% of all new business came from these solicitations. Consider your own business, 20% growth is a number to be proud of. When we put together a list of terms that described their ideal customer, geography never came into the discussion.

For some, geography is a major descriptor, but one size does not fit all. A zip code is not always the most effective way to put together an Ideal Customer list.

When this company looked at the description of their best customers, the number one trait was based on the types of product they manufactured. Not geography. Once they identified this trait, it made it far easier to market to only their ideal customer and stop wasting time knocking on doors of non-ideal customers. Scott could stop replacing his shoes, and he was grateful to us for saving his sole.

Take a look at your favorite customers. Your favorites are the customers who don't feel like work. You enjoy their phone calls, rather than dread having to talk to them. They pay on time, rather than having to be repeatedly invoiced. They're regular clients, and a simple reminder from you is welcomed. They love your product and you don't have to convince them of the benefits. They think your pricing is fair and aren't constantly complaining or comparing you to the cheaper competition. They play an active role in the conversation and aren't defensive when you suggest an idea. They get excited when you bring out something new, rather than make excuses not to see you. It's a relationship, not a transaction.

There are favorite clients and there are clients you would like to fire. Chances are, if you're feeling strained about doing business with a customer; they're feeling the same way. If a little communication can't remedy the situation, chances are, they aren't your ideal customers, and more than likely, you must refer them to someone else.

It's not worth your time to chase around prospects that aren't your ideal customer.

If they give you grief on the front end, you'll end up being further grieved down the road. I received a great piece of advice one day when I was told to "fight my battles on the front end". The logic here is that you won't delay the battle with a customer if it's not the right fit. You can either discover it now, when it's easiest to break free, or later, when feelings get hurt and leave everyone feeling raw from the experience.

It's a bird, it's a plane, it's Super Busy Person!
When it comes to getting things done, we're all Super Heroes.

These days, your prospects are Super Busy. There isn't anyone who isn't, so calling you back, making their next order or in general, staying in touch with you, isn't your prospect's biggest priority. They are busy building their own business; so don't jump to the conclusion that just because a prospect hasn't called you back, they aren't interested. They're probably really interested but they need you to be persistent. In other words, it's up to you to do your job.

"The rock wasn't cut in half because the water was powerful. The rock was cut in half because the water was persistent."

Your ability to bring more customers through your sales process is equal to the amount your customers trust you. They trust you to sell them only products they need. This means, *you will only sell your product to a customer that needs your product.* Your ideal client needs your product, can afford it, and has an emotional desire to do business with you.

Just because someone can fog a mirror does not make him your ideal client.

To put this in perspective, I'll demonstrate with two run-of-the-mill industries, a Chiropractor and a Plumber. Much like you, they have a lot of competition and don't really feel like they have something that sets them apart. Both feel like everyone in the country is their ideal customer because everyone has a spine and everyone has a toilet.

As they begin to build a website, create a social media presence and determine where to advertise, they run into a big dilemma. They don't know who benefits the most from their service.

Men or women, young or old, white collar or blue collar, city or suburbia, family or single, coffee or tea? According to each business owner, it's every one. There's no way to build a marketing plan that caters to everybody.

> *Everyone needs my product.*
> *It's perfect for everyone.*
> *Everyone.*
> *But I can't describe them for you.*

The excuse for not identifying an ideal client is the fear that you will turn business away, and right now, you need every client you can get.

When we started Experience Pros, our answer to "who is our ideal client?" used to be "anybody who will pay me." Another terrible reply is "our ideal client is small to medium-sized companies". That describes no one, ever. I'm betting that not only does it NOT describe an ideal client; it also makes the describer sound desperate and unprofessional.

You need a certain number of more clients and you need to stop wasting your time getting them.

What sets you apart from your competition and ensures that you're not wasting your marketing resources is to identify and market to your ideal client. I want your ideal client to be as unique as possible.

I read about a real estate agent who was kicking her competition in the teeth in a declining real estate market. Everyone around was in dire straights for keeping their doors open, except for this one woman. She catered to a unique clientele.

A Very Unique Clientele

See if you can picture this. She describes her ideal client as a Harley-Davidson® motorcycle-riding Polish Woman.

Now, it doesn't get any clearer than that. You can absolutely create an image in your mind of this woman. It might describe someone you already know or have met. If you ever come across a woman on a hot rod motorcycle with a thick European accent that happens to be in the market for a new home, you would instantly be able to offer her an ideal recommendation. There's only one woman in the world that would get your referral.

She also sells homes for the friends of these women because her service fits a lot of demographics, but her ideal client is her sweet spot and it's where 80% of her business comes from.

That's excellent branding. That's creating word-of-mouth marketing. And that's a success story you can duplicate.

Just because you think everyone can use your product, doesn't mean you should sell it to him or her.

Now, back to our chiropractor friend. He specializes in treating competitive bike racers. Do you know any competitive bike racers? If you meet one who is complaining about his back or achy joints, you know who to refer him to. He advertises on sports shows, in bike shops and in local cycling magazines. He always has a booth at the bike races. He also treats people who don't even own a bike. He treats family members of the bike racers. He treats a lot of people because his service fits a lot of different lifestyles, but his sweet spot is competitive bike racers and that's where 80% of his business comes from.

The plumber created a similar success story.

Our plumber specializes in treating homes for root damage in a specialized part of town where the homes were built during the turn-of-the-century and the hundred-year old trees have an established root system that wreaks havoc on the plumbing.

He puts flyers on the doors in this neighborhood, he places yard signs when he's providing a service and he keeps an extra truck strategically parked nearby, where traffic and visibility in and out of the neighborhood is high. The truck has a vehicle wrap that has a specially branded phone number just for this neighborhood.

He advertises in the local coupon book that targets this neighborhood and has a website that includes this neighborhood in the SEO package (Search Engine Optimization, making sure he gets found by the most popular key words people are searching for). He does business in other neighborhoods, too, but his sweet spot has a zip code that brings him 80% of his business.

Don't be afraid to clearly identify your ideal client. It will clear up so much confusion for you and for your referring clients. They'll be able to clearly identify great prospects for you.

You'll know exactly where to market yourself. You'll be able to create a website that clearly speaks to your prospects hot buttons.

When we're on the air, we've developed a sweet spot for speaking to business owners and entrepreneurs. Every now and then, we get off track and bring in a topic that doesn't perfectly fit. This is when our producer comes to us and reminds us that we have a sweet spot that our listeners depend on.

One of the easiest things to do is stop listening and push the button for a new channel. When we stay on-topic, we speak directly to our ideal clients, in this case, our listeners.

Once you identify your ideal client, you have the ability to filter out the non-ideal clients. This is valuable information. Too often, your time is spent chasing down prospects that will never buy from you. You waste time trying to convince someone that your product is right for him or her. Even if you make the sale, your time and resources are wasted because they took up too much time and most likely won't ever shop with you again because they're not ideal.

This happens a lot when you first open your business doors and you're selling to friends and family. The immediate success is gratifying, but eventually, you need to stop hitting up mom and neighbors and build your multi-million dollar enterprise from a pipeline of ideal clients.

You need to do business with people who like you, trust you and want to refer others to you. Your time is too valuable to just be busy. Busy doesn't pay the bills. Busy doesn't help you reach your goals. Busy, busy, busy doesn't cut it. You need to be productive.

Focus on the right prospects. Put your energy and resources into building a website, business card and packaging that speaks directly to the emotions of your clients, rather than the logics.

Become their favorite and they'll become loyal, braggin' fans.

People do business with people they know, like, and trust.

I specialize in...

Chapter 5
Wear Your Visibility Cloak

Location, location, location. It's the secret sauce to real estate. It's also your secret weapon to building customer relationships. You want to be everywhere your customers are. Think of your brand as Visa®, it's everywhere you want to be. Take lessons and ride on the research of big brands to grow your company. They have an advantage of a large sales force and significant marketing budgets. You too, have a marketing advantage. You have looked every single one of your customers in the eye and shaken their hand. You know them. You have a relationship with them.

The tendency for small business owners is to underestimate that power. Small is only a state of mind. You can be everywhere your customer is, once you start thinking like Visa®.

Big brands have done the research for you and most of it can be found by doing a little homework yourself either at the library, Small Business Development Centers or on the Internet.

I found that Coca-Cola® wants you to see their brand 358 times per day. Per day! Now compare that to your plan of sending out a newsletter once a month. How in the world do you expect to keep up and grow your company with 12 impressions a year, compared to bigger brands vying for the same dollars from your customer? You can't. There's absolutely no comparison.

In advertising, most radio stations will encourage you to invest in a 100-commercial package. The reason is because there are hundreds of other messages targeting your same audience and you need to infiltrate. More, more, more. This is especially important if you're brand new. If no one has heard of you before, you are starting at ground zero to build a reputation for yourself.

Your brand needs to communicate a promise of trust and credibility. The way the brain works, you need to see something twelve times before you begin to remember that you've ever seen it at all. Once you hit the tipping point, is when you start to build on the trust and eventually, that trust turns into business.

Contrast that formula with meeting someone for the first time at a networking event and he or she immediately assumes you'll want to do business with him or her. Fail. Unless I've heard of you before, I won't immediately part with my money, change where I'm currently shopping, and trust you to take care of my needs. Even if I'm completely disgruntled with my current provider, I'm more likely to stay where I'm familiar before switching to some unknown company. Contrary to what customers will tell you, they aren't looking for better, they're looking for familiar. You can be that familiar brand by building a strategic presence.

Be the Visa® for your brand. Choose multiple marketing channels that fit your niche. Most can be free or very low cost. In fact most of your marketing impact can be from activities that only require your time and not your money. Think of networking, social media, blogging, optimizing your key words on search engines and using Google® +, sitting on a board of directors or volunteering for committees, writing articles, and speaking for trade groups.

While setting up your marketing channels, keep your branding consistent by matching up all your promotional materials, and having quality promotional products. As the expert in your industry, you wouldn't print your own business cards on your desktop printer.

A brand new retailer held an open house and invited the local chamber of commerce group. Her clothing store catered to women, so inviting the local women's business groups was targeting her ideal clients.

It was brilliant to host an event, invite her ideal clients and showcase her wares. There were refreshments and prizes. The only thing missing was sales weren't being encouraged. More than that, she let the group know that because she is new, she doesn't have a budget for marketing so she's heavily relying on her customers for word-of-mouth referrals. Seriously? Yes, it's important to let your clients know you appreciate their referrals, and they have the ability to outdo your sales force, once you have a system in place, but is it a smart business plan to hand off the bulk of your marketing to someone who doesn't have an invested interest? If you're struggling and you expect your customers to do what you're not willing to do, you will become an IRS statistic.

Another gal just opened up a fitness center. Because she is also functioning on a minimal budget, she is in the store all day long running low-attended classes and working on paperwork so she can't be out marketing to bring in new clients.

They both ask the same question, "What can I do for free to bring in more clients? I opened up a store, but where do new customers come from?" It's the same question we all find ourselves asking at some point or another. We especially start finding ourselves asking this question when the economy shifts. What worked before doesn't seem to be working anymore. Or what I thought would work, never seemed to really take off.

My friend was into playing an Internet game called FarmVille®. He was so engaged in the game and wanted me to know how much playing the game helped him understand basic business skills. He explained to me that the principles of the game were very similar to real-life business practices. In the game, you have to plant seed, harvest your crops, take the crops to the market to sell, and reinvest your money for new seed.

I wanted to learn more about the marketplace process of the game, since this could turn out to be a great teaching tool for my clients. It wasn't.

In the game, how do the customers learn about the marketplace? How do the customers know when the marketplace is open and what vendors will be there? How do the customers choose your booth versus a competitor's booth?

As a participant of the game, your role was to be the farmer. There was no active role in marketing other than showing up at the market with your basket of goods and the customers showed up, bought everything you had, and at the end of the day, your bank account was full.

I was very frustrated at the concept that the game was teaching that if you have something to sell, customers will show up to buy it. That's what gets entrepreneurs into trouble. Entrepreneurs often mistakenly assume the customers will just show up. But what if they don't?

The Internet offers so many free marketing resources that entrepreneurs undervalue the effort, and therefore, underestimate their own value.

You have to be strategic in keeping your brand in front of your customers around the clock, 24 hours a day. You have to give them a reason to return your phone calls and engage you in an easy conversation that's a win-win for everyone. You need them to refer you, but the only strategy you know is to do a great job and HOPE they refer you.

Without customers, you don't have a multi-million dollar enterprise; you have a hobby. When you search around for free PR and cheap ways to market your company, you undermine your own mindset. Most entrepreneurs keep to the free or low cost marketing for far too long. Their mindset keeps them thinking too small.

You are a multi-million dollar enterprise. Imagine you're about to be endorsed by a major brand. They like your company, they believe in you and they want to endorse you. This happened to my friend, Mary.

Mary was so excited that a major celebrity was endorsing her brand new company. She immediately came up with a marketing strategy to promote the endorsement. This was no time to play small, but to represent her company in a big way.

The thing you need to keep in mind is this: you don't need a celebrity endorsement to get started. You can create all that marketing buzz and PR for yourself, from right where you are. You don't have to wait to be "discovered" to create a fantastic PR campaign. Your existing database creates a far bigger influence in the marketplace because they bring their own trust factor to their key relationships. You don't need to land the big fish in order to reach success, lots of little fish singing your praises is far more lucrative.

Chapter 6
Invitation Marketing

By dividing your sales plan into two phases, you'll always be in either the Invitation Stage or the Follow Up Stage with your contacts. Each quarter, you'll put together an event to promote to your clients. Why an event? Because it changes the conversation 180 degrees: it's not a sales-pitch. Right now, the only conversations you're having with people are sales talk. No one wants to be sold, and people will start to avoid you if you don't have anything of value to add to them.

An event adds value. It makes people feel included. It creates excitement and enthusiasm for your brand, and most importantly, it works on the benefits of sociology. It brings a group of people who are interested in you together in one space. The excitement generated from the people in the room translates to excitement for your brand.

Holding an event lowers people's defenses when it comes to buying. They're in a fun and relaxed setting, so their buying posture relaxes, too.

It gives you a reason to put your brand in front of your customers and keep your brand on the tip of their tongue. It makes it easy for them to share your brand with their friends. It gives them a leg-up on being in-the-know with current events. It helps them answer the question, "what's new?" when they're talking to their friends. Your brand becomes the buzz.

An event ensures retention, referrals and revenue. You have to give your customers a reason to get excited. An event is more exciting than a discount or a sale. Sales are getting to be blasé. Most major retailers know that consumers are responding less and less to the hype of another weekend markdown that is supposedly even better than last weekend's markdowns.

Put your marketing team together and come up with four events. After a few runs at this, you'll discover that you can repeat some of them each year with only a few adjustments to keep them fresh. You can use the seasons, holidays, and piggyback on local events. You can build events around new movies, books, or other celebrity or social news. Partner up with a local charity and help them with their current campaigns. Enter local contests to be the best in your city.

One of our favorites campaigns is to celebrate milestones. Not only does this help us to recognize how much we're doing, it creates credibility and excitement among our audience.

We threw an event when we switched over from Internet to the AM dial and ran a press release along with our other marketing channels.

We just celebrated our 2,000[th] broadcast that could've easily been overlooked if we weren't focused on celebrating milestones. When you start to look for reasons to hold an event, you'll find them.

So often, your company reaches important milestones, yet, you don't share the accomplishment with your customers. These celebrations are built-in trust builders and they increase your credibility and stability in your customer's mind. This is one way to prove to them what a fantastic company you are to work with, and another reason for them to tell others about you.

The concept of marketing doesn't have to be baffling. It can be as simple as Inviting and Following Up.

Once you create a system with four events per year, you'll discover that you're always in one of two stages with your contacts, the Invitation Stage or the Follow Up Stage.

This keeps your pipeline from never going empty.

Super Simple Sales Systems

Having a full pipeline and attracting people to your brand is only part of your success equation. You have to make it super easy for prospects to take the next step into your sales process.

A simple flow chart will put your sales team at ease by creating a duplicable sales process. This means that every customer, every time, has a consistent experience, that no matter who is at the helm taking caring of the customer, the process remains basically the same.

At each interaction, there is a predictable next step. Each step brings your customer through your sales process, and back again for repeat purchases. If it's hard or confusing to do business with you, prospects will shop somewhere else. Review your process to be sure it's sales-friendly.

The founder of the Starbucks® coined the phrase, "We're not in the coffee business, serving people. We're in the people business serving coffee." That means that no matter what industry you're in, you're in the people business.

I read that if radio were invented today, it would be all the rage because of how easily the media interfaces with the on-the-go consumer. You can listen in your car, on your smartphone, at your desk. No matter where you are, you can listen to a radio station in any city or state, thanks to online streaming features and podcasting that's available. You can listen to the radio while doing other things such as driving, working in the yard, catching up on filing and data entry.

No other media can offer that. Television and magazines are limited to having your eyes on the screen, yet radio is far more visual because the listener fills in the images for themselves, therefore, making it so personal to the end listener. It's the Visa® of media.

Stop trying to create another brochure for your business. Instead, create another point of sale to make it easier for your customer to do business with you.

Start considering every point of entry, not as a brochure for your company, but as platform for creating new business. Each point of entry can be a place to create a transaction.

Your business card can be used to create a sale, in exchange for a free cup of coffee, a discount, or an added gift with purchase. Most business cards find their way into the trash because they have no value to them. Unless someone is trying to build up his or her database with new entries, your contact information isn't worth saving when I can easily look you up online.

Your website has multiple opportunities for creating passive revenue streams. Check out some of your favorites from a vendor point of view, and you'll start to see the possibilities.

Besides your main product or service, you can offer pdf downloads, promotional products with your logo and tag line, eBooks, webinars, and how-to videos. You can repackage your products to create a new offer. Most likely, you already have the content and the resources in-house.

The more interactive your website is, the more interesting it is to visit and to invite others to visit. Your website is not a brochure. It's your interactive virtual store.

The end goal is to bring new customers through your sales process.

When you host an event, the end goal is not fill the room with a crowd. The purpose is to introduce prospects to your company and bring them through your sales process. Most companies open the doors and expect the customers to take the next step. Too often, a vendor will host an event and complain a few months later that they didn't get any new business from it. Really? What did you do to create any new business?

You need to create a call-to-action at the event.

You need to follow up afterwards.

During the event, you need to showcase your benefits rather than expecting the tray of cheese and crackers to do it for you.

You need to offer bonuses that create a sense of urgency, and send your guests off with a token that continues to remind them of your brand.

All the marketing in the world will ensure that people have heard of you and bring them *TO* your sales process. It's up to you to take them *through* your sales process.

6-Week Invitation Stage

Week One – Announce "Save The Date" on social media and in conversations.

Week Two and Three – Send out invitations. Use email, social media and even the US mail.

Week Three-Five - Create awareness of your event. Make a list of 10 marketing channels to use:

Facebook Event, Eventbrite, Meetup, Website Landing Page, Special URL (website name), Live Videos, Hang Posters/Flyers, Pass out postcards, Write Personal Emails, Send a Newsletter, use your CRM email and Affiliate Emails.

Add into your Email Signature and update your Voicemail to include the event.

The Point through every step is to continue to invite people through your sales process. Keep that in mind so you don't get distracted from your purpose.

Create sales conversations by asking questions that highlights their needs and get them to your next step of the sales cycle. This isn't pushy or sales-pitching. You're creating an avenue for the sales conversation to happen.

Week Five - Collect confirmations by making phone calls.

This is the most important step in the Invitation Stage. You've put your brand on the top of their mind, and they are thinking about you in positive way. They're remembering how great your customer service is. They remember why they bought from you before, or why they forgot to call you. Allow for the sales conversation to happen.

Keep in mind, they will likely say no to your invitation. Remember, they're busy and it's okay for them to say no. In fact, it's almost preferred. You can't entertain hundred people at your event very well, so this is the conversation that opens up a new dialogue.

They will be surprised to hear from you. Surprised and delighted. They may be a little embarrassed that they haven't reached out to you in so long, so be sure to put them at ease. This is the phone call where magic happens.

Magic happens when they say, "Thank you for calling, I've been thinking about doing business with you again."

Or, this happens:

"Thank you, I can't attend your event, but I have a referral for you."

In every case, something positive comes out of the phone call. I promise. This is the part of the process that surprises my clients the most. The reason it's so productive is because you've primed the pump with value before you ever call.

Multiple impressions improve the response you'll get. The more impressions you make of wanting to add value, before asking for a sale, greatly increases their likelihood of always taking your phone call, and responding to your requests.

Don't skip this step, and don't rush to get to this step. This is where you'll discover the true value of the Invitation Stage.

At the event, be sure to create an incentive for people to make a quick and easy decision to say yes to your purchase. Gift-with-purchase, today-only bonuses, incentives, discounts, and extras all create a sense of urgency. Allow for the energy of the room to create new prospects. Celebrating the one's that say on the spot encourages others to jump in, too.

Celebrate your VIP's who are in attendance. Recognize current and past customers. Everyone loves to be part of a social group and they love to be recognized, even if it's just a round of applause. Don't underestimate the power of applause for them.

Action Step: Have order forms on-hand to make it easy for people to get started right now, without having to take too much time away from the event or other conversations going on. Have a calendar available to make appointments on the spot. At the very least, put their business card in a special location to ensure immediate follow up action.

Without customers, you don't have a multi-million dollar business, you have an expensive hobby.

Chapter 7
Follow Up Stage

Every interaction with your customer is the gateway to the next interaction with your customer. The courting of a new customer is fairly expected and built in. You'll call. You'll email. You'll drop off samples and present them with raving testimonials. You pretty much turn over every loose stone to get them to buy from you. But after the sale, this is where extreme customer service needs to kick in.

Your customer doesn't expect to hear from you again until you're in a crunch or having a promotion and you need them to "Buy Now". All of a sudden, it's an emergency to get them to purchase. Don't miss out! Today Only! Freak out your customer and back them into an impulse purchase!

Yes, this can be a viable business option, but it's not sustainable. You aren't after satisfied customers, you want loyal customers who shop with you regularly and invite their friends to do the same. The number one proven method for increasing sales and retaining customers is having a consistent follow up strategy.

The number one proven system that is missing in struggling companies is the lack of a consistent follow up strategy.

If you follow up with your customers, they will think of you more often. If you follow up with your customers, they will shop with you more often. If you follow up with your customers, they will tell others about you, and they do it more often.

The average company brings in 30% more customers every year, yet they lose 30% of their customer base out the back door due to lack of a retention strategy.

They never hear from you. Or worse, the only time they hear from you is when you want them to open up their checkbook (or virtually swipe their card). That's not a relationship, that's a transaction.

The very best flyer to send to your customers isn't a postcard, though I really like postcards. Postcards are an ideal flyer to send to prospect and current customers, if they include a reason to hold on to it, such as helpful tips or a sporting calendar, they will be tacked up on a bulletin board for all the world to see. If it's simply an oversized business card, don't waste your money. It will get pitched in the recycling bin faster than you can say print-your-own-postage.

Take the time to make it valuable. Include a gift with purchase, or a special incentive. Add a checklist of the *7 Top Ways To Improve Their Situation or Solve Their Pain* – and be sure that it ties directly to your brand.

The very best flyer to send to your customers isn't a coupon, though coupons can create a sense of urgency getting your customers back in the door again.

If you're going to slash your prices, make it worthwhile for everyone, including your time and energy to print and promote. 15% off rarely creates frenzy out the door. $100.00 off will stir the crowd, but you need to stay in business.

Every grocery chain in town offers a weekly "loss leader" in order to drive customers into the store. They entice you with 99 cents a pound for a chicken, in hopes that while you're there, you'll stock up on other essentials, too. Without the bonus of the deal, you may shop somewhere else, or not at all.

You can duplicate a "Loss Leader" with your own campaigns, as long as you have other items that your customers might also like, *as long as they're there.*

The Very Best Promotional Item

The very best promotional item you can mail to your customer to strengthen your relationship with them, and to keep your brand top-of-mind, is a handwritten note card. Not an e-card. Not a post card, a handwritten thank you card. However, you'll immediately undo the sentiment by including the words "By the way, I'd appreciate your referrals." Keep the focus of the card on your gratitude, without an expectation of anything in return.

A handwritten note card doesn't require a special occasion.

A handwritten note card can be written for no reason at all, other than, "I really appreciate you and I'm grateful that you bring your business to me." You don't need to wait for a campaign, you can write one today.

Handwritten notecards are often the first item opened when filtering through a stack of mail. Handwritten note cards are often displayed. Handwritten note cards are shared. Handwritten note cards are saved. Even our out-going President writes a hand written card for the incoming President of the United States.

Handwritten notecards are the best value you can invest in to connect with your customers.

6-Week Follow Up Stage

Immediately after your event, your pipeline goes into your Follow Up Stage.

Write handwritten thanks you – even for people that didn't come. In this digital age, this is a sure-fire way to stand out above your competition. Imagine receiving a Thank You Card for something you didn't do. It leaves quite the impression, and strengthens relationships. It puts people at ease for saying no to you, encouraging them that there's still room to say yes in the future.

I like to encourage you to send a Thank You Card to someone who called on you, but decided to buy from someone else. If the person they bought from didn't send a Thank You Card after the purchase, who do you think will still win their on-going referral business? Yes, it will be you.

Week One thru Three - Meet with qualified prospects. Put it on your calendar to follow up with the people you had conversations with. Don't wrap up the event without follow up. The ball is in your court to turn these excited, interested prospects into customers. Make phone calls, send text messages, set appointments, and take them through your sales process.

Week Three thru Six – Follow up with everyone else. Give them a few weeks to marinate on what you're offering. Send something of value through email such as Top Tips, Current Trends, or Hot Items.

By hosting 4 events a year, you'll keep your brand top-of-mind. You'll keep your pipeline full. You'll celebrate your VIP's and give your contacts a reason to share your service. You'll get a chance to spread your influence to people you haven't yet met. You'll have a reason to reach out to cold leads, warm leads and super hot ones, too.

Throughout the entire 12-weeks, you're creating customer-conversations that lead to sales. You're not waiting for the event to happen to create the sales. Every step of the way, you're creating an opening for the sales conversation to happen. Every email, every text, and every phone call has the potential to turn into a sale by keeping the line of communication open. You're not calling to push a sale, you're calling to invite or follow up.

This is how you get passed the gate-keeper. This is how you get people to take your calls and to return your calls. You're adding value.

Always Be Adding Value

Chapter 8
Become a Radio Star

You probably do the same thing a lot of other people do. Maybe you sell insurance or financial services. Maybe you're a life coach or a health coach. Maybe you sell marketing or website services. No matter what, your potential clients probably hear what you do and immediately lump you with anyone else they know that does that, too. Your job is to stand out. A great way to stand out is to be viewed as the expert in your field.

We're going to take you from being in the middle of the crowd to the top of the pack. You're going to be viewed as *The Expert*, and you're going to back it up with the goods. It takes more than putting the word Expert on your LinkedIn profile; you've got to have some real substance behind it. My friend, Bill Walsh says to put your finger to your temple and say this out loud, "My knowledge has value." That knowledge is your Intellectual Property, and you need to share it. You're going to give some of it away, and you're going to monetize some of it.

Specialists are worth more

When you go to a doctor who is a specialist, they often come with both higher credibility and a higher price tag than a general practitioner. You might be a life coach, but you probably have something more significant that you specialize in. You might sell insurance, but you probably have a sweet spot for either one of your products or a certain demographic.

When you review your Ideal Customer, your specialty can focus on them. For example: Retirement Specialist for the Millennial Generation, Nutrition Specialist for Teachers, and Insurance Specialists for Creative Arts. Think of your demographic as small enough for people to recognize themselves or someone they know, yet large enough for you to mass market to.

Action Step: Add your specialty to your LinkedIn profile, email signature and business card.

Finally, write your own book

It's easier than ever to become a published author. When I published my first book in 2009, I only knew of one other self-published author. Now, everyone can publish. Don't put it off any longer. Take some of your TV watching time and write your book. You can re-purpose your blogs, any presentations you've done, or transcribe your recorded videos and compile them into a 150-page book.

If you haven't done it before, let me remind you, it's your first book. You'll learn everything you need to learn along the way, and once you've written the first book, every other book will be far easier to do. Let's get this first one done so you can move on.

Speaking To Build Your Brand

Your business is going to grow to a point where you'll recognize that there's not enough time in a day to pitch your product one on one. You're going to have to speak to an audience, and the best way to speak to an audience is on the phone doing a radio interview. Even if you're nervous about public speaking, you've probably been really comfortable speaking on the phone since you were a kid.

Being interviewed on the radio is just like talking on the phone with friends. The interviewer is very interested in what you have to say. They want to listen and they want to learn from you. Plus, you're in the comfort of your own home or office. You can even be wearing your favorite bathrobe, if you like.

Tips for Your Radio Interview

Use a landline whenever possible. The quality and consistency from your smartphone isn't the same. If you don't have one, find one.

Be sure there's nothing else going on around you during the interview so you can focus. If you don't plan to avoid interruptions, you didn't plan this phone call. Professionals plan ahead. We don't want to hear your car alarm, dogs barking, doorbells ringing, or timers going off. It distracts from your brilliance. Bring your A-game.

Increase your energy. Move around to create some blood flow, but not so much that you're out of breath.

Smile, laugh and put yourself in a great mood before starting. Your enthusiasm is contagious, but so is your bad mood. Even if you've just been given some truly bad news, you can trick your brain into delivering an energetic interview.

Don't cancel, don't reschedule, and don't miss it. Be sure to keep track of time zones when scheduling your interview, especially with Daylight Savings Time. Not everyone turns clocks forward and back. Your host and their production team has only scheduled you and for this interview and will be scrambling to back fill. They are prepared for this, but they are counting on your courtesy. Failing to plan is planning to fail.

Schedule 4 Radio Interviews This Year

Just like you're using events to grow your pipeline, use your radio interviews to grow your database and create marketing buzz.

Create four working titles for your interviews:

1. Launch of Your New Book Title– use your radio interview to coincide with the release of your new book.
2. Top Tips that serve your audience.
3. Things to Avoid or Shouldn't Do in order to…(your specialty here)
4. How (your target audience) is Getting Ahead

For example:
1. Release of new book: Jumpstart For Business, How to Turn your Slow Months into Your Best Months.
2. 7 Ways to bring in more sales this quarter.
3. How to avoid the small business pitfalls and keep your competition from stealing your market share.
4. How small business owners are creating million dollar enterprises.

At the same time you create your interview titles, you're also going to create a Tip Sheet or Recorded Video to match. This can be a one-sheet that is downloaded from your website, or a 5-7 minute video with the same tips, in exchange for their email address.

Build a Better Landing Page

To make things super simple for the radio audience, create an easy to remember URL – website name – to send the listeners to, especially if your name has multiple spelling options or may be a little tricky.

Here' the litmus test: If you're often spelling or repeating your website name to folks, grab something easier that matches your brand and direct it back to your landing page where people are getting your free offer.

For example, Angel Tuccy is always mispronounced or misspelled. The URL JumpstartForBusiness.com is way easier to remember and to spell.

Mix and Match

Every time you speak, you have a free offer for listeners. Mix and match your titles. If you're speaking on *Top Tips*, give away your free download of *Things to Avoid*. If you're talking about *How to Get Ahead*, give away the recorded video of your *Top Tips*. You can even offer free electronic versions of your books, either the entire book or certain chapters.

Use one radio title and one free download for each quarter and you now have an entire yearlong content calendar for doing radio interviews.

Reach out to Hosts

Thanks to the Internet, everyone you want to be connected to can be found online. Everyone has a profile somewhere.

Action Step: Do a search on LinkedIn, search the podcasts on YouTube, and sign up for the site called HARO (Help A Reporter Out) and you'll find the shows that offer the best fit for being interviewed. Connect with Experience Pros for being interviewed.

Each of these sites will give you plenty of opportunities to be interviewed. Plan to conduct at least one interview every month, move into once a week to create your expert image.

You'll send the producer or host an email inquiry with the words "Guest Opportunity – and your topic" in the subject line of your email. You'll provide a list of 5-7 questions for your hosts to use a guideline. Relax and follow your host's lead. They are the experts on their audience's expectations, so go with it.

They may not provide you with the audio file afterwards, so be sure to grab a recording of it yourself, if you want to share it afterwards.

Don't keep it a secret

Every time you speak, make pre-announcements. Feature the programs to your database and on your social sites. This is a great way to highlight your expertise and create curiosity. Your fans will tune in just to hear what you have to share, and it puts your brand back in front of them.

Take pictures of you on the phone, or wearing a headset. Share the cover of your book. Share the free download of the content you're sharing in order to grow your email list. Bang your own drum until others take over.

Chapter 9
Share Kindness

Your business is made up of people with busy lives, fears, hopes and big dreams. Everyday, they struggle with challenges, just like you do.

The world can be a mean, dark and ugly place. Everyday we battle with strangers on the highway and people who criticize and complain. Bad news and gossip travel too easily and infiltrate well-meaning companies and families. People feel lost, invisible and unheard. The antidote to all that is angry and dark in the world is to share kindness.

We say that Kindness Is So Simple, and everyday we encourage our listeners to give someone a 20-second K.I.S.S. Your smile, holding a door open, saying thank you and every day, looking at your database and being truly grateful for all that you've been given, is the act that will change your mindset into growing a multi-million dollar enterprise.

Business is not rocket-science, it's people science. Your company has the foundation for being a multi-million-dollar enterprise, but only if you treat it that way. Give it the attention it deserves and the rewards will far outweigh the sacrifices.

Put what's truly important into your calendar. Take time each day to appreciate all that you've been given and take advantage of the time you have.

Live well. Live the life you dream of living.

Laugh much. Find joy in the small things. Appreciate life for its laughter.

Love much. Love makes the world go round. When you love what you do, who you spend your time with, you'll find that time is what you make it to be.

Bonus Chapter Excerpt from
Lists That Saved My Business

In a market full of overwhelming choices, competitive prices and message overload, it seems that businesses are finding it more and more difficult to connect with customers in a new and fresh way. Is bigger and faster always better? In a rushed society, sometimes we forget to slow down and realize that our customers are real people, just like us.

When you stop and take a deep breath, you'll be able to hear the heartbeat of your business: it's your customers. When you spend some time actually listening to your customers, focusing on the people and not just the sale, you can connect and create a loyal customer base that brags about your service. The key to extreme customer service is old-fashioned really; stay in touch with your customers.

Pauline Szafranski, the vice president of marketing for Lotus Concepts agrees that business is going back to a grassroots mentality. "Everything was over-the-top, big and impersonal for a decade," says Szafranski. "The backlash has made people pick up the phone instead of emailing, write thank you notes, and take time for a business lunch instead of faxing over contracts."

Today's consumers don't want to be bombarded with sales pitches. They want to feel valued and important. Finding a way to reach your customers without interrupting them or intruding on them will help them feel like they are participants, rather than being manipulated into a purchase.

To help you stay in touch with your customers, we put together nine protocols that will connect you with them, create extreme customer service and release loyal ambassadors for your brand into the world.

#1 – EMAIL

Email is the most crowded and overused, but also the most expected form of communication. So if you're going to send an email, make it personal and *never* send spam or junk mail.

> Always ask permission to place someone on your newsletter mailing list. If you don't know the person well enough to pick up the phone and call them, they don't belong on your list. If it's someone you know, who knows you, or has an inkling of interest, then you're probably okay, but we would still recommend asking. If your relationship is too weak to ask, then you are at risk to losing them to your competition.

There's a reason consumers call it "junk" mail. Don't send junk. Ever. Use email to send a personal note and share information.

TIPS FOR SENDING EFFECTIVE EMAILS

Always include your contact information and logo in your email signature. If you send something worthwhile, the hope is that your message will be forwarded. Make sure people can contact you.

Do not use email to make a decision or conduct a conversation; too much is left up to interpretation.

Keep the subject line of your email current with the discussion thread. Change the subject box, for example, if the conversation has moved away from the conference that is taking place next week to the promotional products for the next trade show.

Be clear about whether or not you expect a reply.

#2 - TELEPHONE

The telephone, which can sometimes be viewed as weighing 100 pounds, is one of your greatest links to building rapport. In the age of quick emails, the phone can be a welcome channel for making solid connections. If you need a quick response, the telephone can often be quicker than email.

There are times when you need to make sales calls, but we like to think of your telephone more as an additional way to connect with your customers. Don't always use the telephone to make a sales pitch. Sometimes, your customers just need to hear your voice. These conversations can often take on a life of their own and when you listen intently, you might just learn something that helps you help them.

Tips for Leaving Effective Phone Messages

Leave a brief, yet clear message with your name and phone number, even if you're sure they have caller ID. Tell the recipient who you are, why you are calling, and how to respond. We've had phone messages where the name of the caller was fuzzy and we didn't recognize the number. These phone calls don't get returned quickly – if at all.

Keep your messages brief. Think about what you want to say before you dial. More often than not, you will be sent to voicemail, so be prepared to leave a short message, not your entire sales pitch.

Leave your phone number at the beginning and at the end of the phone message.

Avoid leaving this message: "Hi, it's me. Call me back." Unless you are calling your very best golfing buddy, who knows exactly why you are calling because you have been best friends since the third grade... this is *not* an effective phone message.

Use your own answering message to create a memory. We already know you that you can't take our call right now, because we got your voicemail. So use your message to bring a smile to my face instead. We call it "disrupting their complacency." If you can keep your customers out of "voice message coma", you can get them to talk about your voicemail message and even get others to call you and keep sharing it. Let your next caller feel compelled to tell two friends...and so on, and so on.

Here's a great example: *"Do you hear that sizzle? Can you smell that aroma? I'm in the kitchen cooking up something delectable for lunch today. Place your catering order and I'll cook lunch for you tomorrow."*

Keep your answering message short, but professionally interesting.

Return phone messages. Call your customers back every time they call you... preferably before the close of the business day.

#3 – U.S. Mail

Sending a handwritten letter, card or note can go a long way in creating long-term customers, and offering extreme customer service. You can almost guarantee that your handwritten card will be opened, especially if it's personal. Handwritten cards never lose their luster, and a personalized note can make a powerful and positive impact on your customer.

We keep a memo board of the cards we receive, and it's about time for a second board! Sometimes the best pick-me-up on a rough day is to read a friendly note from someone who took time out of his or her busy day to say, "You matter". We all struggle everyday, and a genuine note can really mean a lot. It only takes you a few minutes, but the impact is far greater. If you need some tips on what to say, visit a greeting card website or ExperiencePros.com for starters. If you write something genuine and heartfelt, it will be right.

Tips for Writing Cards

Make it personal and hand-written.

Include your logo on the envelope or stamp.

Remember birthday cards, anniversary cards, get well cards, thank you cards and notes of appreciation.

When the postmaster raises prices, send your customers a page of 2-cent stamps.

Send cards every day to people you meet and always send a thank you after the sale.

Cards are often shared and displayed for others to take notice, whereas a note on letterhead is typically filed or even tossed.

#4 - Face-to-Face

When your customer is involved in the buying process, you are focused on offering great customer service. But, what are you doing for them *after* the sale or before they've decided to purchase again? A client doesn't care how much you know until they know how much you care.

Tips for Face-to-Face Interaction

Drop in and visit in between appointments or when you happen to be in the area. This gesture goes a long way in creating a genuine customer connection. Bringing treats ensures that the office staff looks forward to your "drop-in".

Set up a coffee date. We like to hold what we call, "non-dinner dinner parties". Like many people in business, we found that coffee meetings were well suited to our business, and allowed an opportunity for us to get to know others, as well as them to get to know us. We also discovered that having five or six coffee meetings each week was really eating into our available time.

In an effort to replicate the value of a dinner party where twelve to fourteen guests get together to meet one another, we decided to host "non-dinner dinner parties" and we set them up like this: Each week we schedule a time to meet someone for coffee. This could be a current client, a potential client, or someone we're just starting to get to know. Leading up that coffee date, when we receive other invitations for coffee, we add them to the existing coffee meeting. The result is five or six people having coffee together. The meetings are very dynamic. In many cases these people might never otherwise meet, and the outcome is refreshing. If you don't have a lot of time to set up three to five coffee meetings per week, the "non-dinner dinner party" is just for you.

Give them leads. Referrals from you are a great way to add intrinsic value in your customer's mind. Giving leads to your customers keeps you on the top of their list of people to call, and that's always a good thing. You might just discover that goodwill is reciprocal.

Ask them how you can serve them better. Rather than sending a generic survey that doesn't really give you the answers you're looking for, ask the real questions face-to-face. More than their words, you'll get a truer response from their facial expressions and body language. If you can help your customer to know that you're listening, you can make real changes that will impact them immediately – and that level of concern will help keep you on the top of their list of quality people doing quality business.

> Create a conversation and ask your customers, "What do you want me to KEEP doing, to STOP doing or to START doing?" Then listen and respond appropriately. Spend time talking with your customers about how you can serve them better, and ask them why they chose you over someone else.

Meeting with your customers face-to-face will help you learn more about their needs, create conversation and bring out solutions. Customers respond favorably when you care enough to spend some time with them. To create extreme customer service, you must care about your customers as people.

Memories are built face-to-face. If you're going to offer extreme customer service, you have to create a memory for your customer to talk about. You need to convert the buying process into a memorable experience. Do something for your customers that they can't expect anywhere else. The goal is to get your customers to brag about you.

Your customers will rarely be more excited about your brand than you are, so you need to be positively contagious and enthusiastic.

#5 - INVITATIONS

Inviting your customers to an event is a great way to re-connect. If it's been a while since they've seen you, heard from you, or purchased from you, invite them to an event and you can rekindle that connection.

Tips for Using Invitations to Stay In Touch

Plan an event of your own, or invite customers to an event that is already happening. Take advantage of the events your community puts together and never go anywhere with your passenger seat empty. Always invite and take along a customer or two.

An invitation is a non-threatening approach to building extreme customer service. It's also a great way to create a dialogue with potential customers.

Match your own passion and be creative. Invite your customers to something you enjoy – and better yet – something you know they enjoy, too. Sporting, cultural, and civic events are going on in your town every week. Check out your local trade magazine or newspaper and plan ahead.

An even better way to get customers through your door and in front of your brand is to create your own gala. Celebrate a milestone, host a fundraiser, or make up any excuse to pull people together. Mix and Mingle Mondays, Trendy Tuesdays, and Wake-Up Wednesdays are creative places to start. Look at the upcoming movies and host a pre-show party. Throw a celebration for the hot trends happening in your industry, and you'll have a never-ending supply of reasons to pull people together.

If you haven't had a ribbon cutting or milestone celebration this year, join your local chamber of commerce and get on their calendar. This is a great way to announce your presence in your community, even if you've already been in business for eight years.

Make the presentation as special as you can. You don't have to spend a lot of money, but you do have to spend some time planning out the details and inviting your guests to show up. Invitations, balloons, door prizes and refreshments that show off your theme or color scheme can turn a ho-hum month into a line of people that are reminded of your brand and who want to do business with you.

Secure the event in your customer's memory with a memento of the occasion. Just like souvenirs or vacation photos, a promotional item that complements the occasion will trigger your customer's memory of you long after the event is over.

Spend time doing what you enjoy with people that you enjoy. You will create very loyal customers when you spend time together. If you are hosting an event, incorporate others to help with the work so that you can spend time mingling with your guests. You will discover many stories that will strengthen your customer relationships.

#6 – FOLLOW-THROUGH

Every customer interaction is an opportunity to re-engage your customer in conversation or bring them further into your sales process. Once you develop a strategic follow-through plan that is automatic and consistent, you will see an increase in sales and customer interaction that is brought forward by your customer, rather than by you. Lost sales are hinged on the lack of follow-through in your planning. Much like your golf swing or tennis serve, the ball goes farther when you follow through. Too often, sales grow cold and money is left on the table when you fail to follow-through with your customers.

Tips for an Effective Follow-Through Plan

Follow up every conversation, email, or newsletter. There should be a constant conversation that is developed through your automatic follow through system. Just as an example: Each conversation should be followed through with an email. Each email response should be followed through with another email or perhaps, a phone call. Each newsletter should be followed through with a phone call or a post card.

When you have an automatic plan for response, you'll never have to wonder if your clients have fallen through the proverbial cracks of being too busy to follow-through. Sure, it takes time, but what else are you doing that is more important than taking care of your customers? The plus side of all of this is that once you have a system in place, you can delegate it and outsource it, because you will be adding new staff to help take care of the customers.

Automatic is not the same as "automated". With an automatic system, you automatically know what step comes next and you personally follow through. You never have to answer for, or make excuses for a real person reaching out to connect with your customers. On the other end of the spectrum, "automated" refers to having a computer-generated follow-through system that isn't personal, and that often ends up causing more frustration for the customers. This causes frustration for your staff as well, for having to answer the question, "Why can't I get a real person to help me?"

When you keep in touch with your customers, they remember to do business with you *and* they tell others to do the same. The key is to stay on their mind, and a satisfactory sales experience will *not* do the trick. Satisfied customers shop around. Satisfied customers are easily swayed away by the competition, referrals from their own friends, or convenience. Unless you keep your brand fresh in your customer's memory, someone else will reap the next purchase.

> Don't let neglect be the reason your customers shop around. Be consistent. Let your customers hear from you all year long, not just when its time to purchase.

Here is a great way to follow through with that customer who was shopping around but purchased somewhere else: Send them a handwritten note card thanking them for the opportunity to offer them a price quote. Most likely, the company they chose didn't even thank them for their business, and here you are with a note card with a handwritten sentiment that says you care and that you hope they were well served.

Who do you think they will talk about? YOU! Who do you think will get their referral business, even though they didn't purchase from you? YOU! Who do you think they will turn to when things go awry and they need help fast? It will be you! Following through builds your business in ways that nothing else will.

#7 - Rewards

Give your customers something they weren't expecting. Reward your customers just for sharing your name. This is a behavior that you want your customers to repeat over and over again; so rewarding them for doing it is a really good idea. It's exciting when someone sends you a lead. You can encourage them to do it again and again with a little bit of behavioral reinforcement – but not in a typical "referral program" sort of way.

Tips for Rewarding your Customers

A typical "referral program" is when you reward the referring party *after* a transaction has taken place with a bonus of some sort. On the surface, this seems like a good idea. Maybe you've been the recipient of such a referral program or you've read about other companies who offer something similar.

If you pay someone for referring a customer to you once the transaction is over, that qualifies as a "commission", not as a referral reward. Your new customer may begin to wonder if the referral was genuine, or did they just get sucked-in to help make someone a little cash on the side.

It is not up to your customers to make the sale for you – that's *your* job. You simply want them to send potential customers your way. Whether or not they actually purchase is irrelevant when paying out a true referral reward.

You want to reward the behavior of the referral; "Tell people about me. Make an introduction, and help me get the word out that I exist."

Instead of paying out a $50.00 bonus once a transaction has occurred, try taking that same $50.00 and invest in ten $5.00 gifts. These can be coffee mugs with your logo, specialty items that match your branding, movie tickets or gift cards to the local coffee shop.
Now, instead of paying out one commission for one referral, you get to pay out ten times. Watch how much quicker your referrals come in! We like to hand out gift cards anytime someone introduces us to someone new. These are people we might not have otherwise met, and they are being brought to us with a glowing introduction. We definitely want to reward that!

Whether or not a sale ever takes place is up to us, and is determined by the timing and needs of the new contact. But no matter what, we want to reward the introduction, so we hand out gift cards (we often keep one or two with us) or we send them in the mail along with a handwritten thank you card.

#8 – REPEAT RECEIPTS

Rewarding your existing customers has an overwhelmingly positive impact on both your customers *and* your team. Everyone gets in on the fun and excitement – and the energy creates a buzz for your brand. Repeat Receipts can do that for you.

Tips for Repeat Receipts

Target your existing customers – at the cash register, at the door, when they check out.
Hand out rewards to entice them to come back the very next day or the very next week. Encourage the behavior you're after. You want them to return quickly and be so excited that they tell other people about it.

Use what you've already got. The little plastic pizza piece that keeps the cheese from sticking to the pizza box can be redeemed the next day for a smoking' hot deal. Michael's prints a 40% off coupon on their cash-register receipts. Kohl's gives you a $10.00 voucher for every $50 spent.

Never let your customer leave without an enticement to get them right back. Otherwise, when do you plan to see them again? Put a date on it.

#9 – Advertise

You've heard of Coke and Pepsi. You could knock on one hundred doors and find out that everyone has heard of these companies. You've heard of State Farm Insurance, Chase Bank, and Oprah Winfrey.

You've heard of them because you keep seeing them on television, reading about them in newspapers and seeing their ads in magazines.

Companies that advertise become familiar to their audience. Familiarity creates a sense of credibility and trust. Advertising warms your marketing and sales efforts. It doesn't replace word-of-mouth marketing; it compliments it. Advertising is a way to leverage your efforts so your customers see your brand, even when you're not there.

Pete Blackshaw says that the radio and television ads that reap the highest attention are for brands with great website strategies along with their advertising. "Doritos, Federal Express, Budweiser, GoDaddy® and every major television and cable network have integrated their websites to keep their advertising more engaging."

Pepsi® ran an experiment where they dropped their television ads in the Super Bowl to focus on Internet advertising and social media. Blackshaw suggests that companies can't afford to abandon advertising on radio and television completely.

Pepsi® didn't stop all of their television advertising; but they *enhanced* it by doing something different and then tying that change to another form of marketing.

Tips for Advertising

Start with your FRANC™ circle. (Friends, Relatives, Associates, Neighbors/Networks & Customers) Who do you know that produces a magazine, or has connections for radio advertising? Does your trade association offer advertising to your favorite customers? Most national companies that advertise on the radio are based in the hometown of the radio personalities that they started with. Start with whom you know.

Focus on reaching your favorite customers. You can ask your current customers to help create your ads. You can run a contest as a great campaign, and you'll have several options to choose from.

Advertising isn't just for television. Consider magazines, radio, billboards, and community events. Let your current customers know about your ads and where to find them. They'll feel like they've chosen the right company because you're obviously going to be around to take care of them for a while.

Use the Internet. It's where so many eyes are. Don't underestimate the power of Internet advertising. A company that makes cupcake stands started with Internet advertising and created a quarter-million dollar company in their first year.

Post your ads on your website. Include extras like outtakes, bloopers and extended versions. Customers like to feel as if they know a secret, so include behind-the-scenes pieces and scarcely known trivia.

Blog about your ads. Include links to find your ad. Make it easy for browsers to share your ad with others with the click of a button.

Blackshaw shares the story of how even major advertisers can sometimes forget to focus on their customers. "When General Motors wanted to create their new advertisement for the Chevy Tahoe, they partnered with *The Apprentice* television show. GM encouraged the show's participants to create their own television ads. While this campaign gained a lot of media attention, it didn't translate into customer loyalty, or even a boost in sales.

GM missed the number one rule in advertising. The contest wasn't focused on their target market: Chevy Tahoe drivers. Most of the ads created were by people who had never purchased or even driven the cars. As a result, the ads lacked the genuine passion and enthusiasm that sends customers running into dealerships."

Focus on speaking to your favorite customers and don't quit too soon. Often, when people start advertising, they expect an immediate return on their investment. In most cases, it takes some time to create trust and familiarity before a customer will buy-in to your brand. They are learning about you, and getting to know you.

When we started our radio show, we thought that our advertisement for Experience Pros University would fill a new class every week. It was professionally produced with Angel's voice and a beautiful musical background. We didn't get our first new student from that ad until six months after it started running. The temptation was strong to pull the ad and say, "it didn't work". It does work. Especially when it's combined with other methods of marketing. General Douglas MacArthur says, "Quitting wrinkles the soul." Stay the course. It's worth it.

In business, if you treat customer service as a hobby and don't commit to the daily care and feeding of the heartbeat of your business, then the only heartbeat you will be hearing will be your own.

Your customers are waiting to hear from you. Don't let them down. Your attention may surprise them and they will tell someone about it. If they talked about you once, you can get them to do it again... provided you treat them right.

List for Staying In Touch with Customers

1. Email

2. Telephone

3. U.S. Mail

4. Face-to-Face

5. Invitations

6. Follow Through

7. Reward Referrals

8. Repeat Receipts

9. Advertise

--Read more of *Lists That Saved My Business* by downloading the eBook. --

About The Author

Angel Tuccy is the host of 2 daily radio shows in Denver, Colorado. She's conducted over 5,000 interviews on the Experience Pros Radio Show. She's been trailblazing for small businesses since 2009. She was named Inspirational Leader of the Year by the SMDCC Women In Leadership, Innovative Business of the Year by the Highlands Ranch Chamber, and Best Morning Radio Show 3 years in a row. Angel is the best selling author of Lists That Saved My Life and Lists That Saved My Business. She sits on the board of directors for Bridge of Hope, is the Past Chairman of the Highlands Ranch Chamber and she is the founder of the professional women's group called Ladies Who Lunch. She loves to write, read and travel with her family. Her Angel and her husband, Jay are the parents of three young adults.

Also by Angel Tuccy

Lists That Saved My Life
(December 2009)

Lists That Saved My Business
(August 2010)

Sex, Drugs & Rock N Roll,
3 Keys For A Healthier Lifestyle
(November 2010)
With Dr. Nick Caras

SUPER-Marketing - Audio
(December 2010)

Mommy Has Lots To Do
(February 2011)
With Alycia Tuccy

Chase Your Dreams Without
Messing Up Your Manicure
(April 2011)

www.ingramcontent.com/pod-product-compliance
Lightning Source LLC
Chambersburg PA
CBHW071211240526
45470CB00018B/1703